a mountain and a guitar —
which plays which
as the moon rises

Also by Thomas and Karen Fitzsimmons

THE RED CLAY DISH

Celebrations

Poems ... Thomas Fitzsimmons
Art ... Karen Fitzsimmons

KATYDID BOOKS
Santa Fe
2013

KATYDID BOOKS

#1 Balsa Rd., Santa Fe, New Mexico 87508
sframbler@gmail.com

ISBN 978-0-942668-02-5

Produced in the United States of America by
KT DID Productions.

First Edition

Thank you once again, Pieter

Contents

This old man's haikai do not intend to follow old master Basho's style. I just go by my own will and enjoy the different atmospheres of yesterday and today. There are no gateways to haikai. There is only the haikai gateway itself.

Yosa Buson, 1716-1784

water brings the birds
to the Red Clay Dish — the birds
bring the poems

The Red Clay Dish

cock calls the dawn
up through moonlight —
time changes color

jewel-breasted Flicker
catches the sun — dips it
into the Red Clay Dish

sun on snow pops
every wrinkle, crag, and gorge
on San Pedro peak

the Garden Shrine floats
in a lake of silence —
lone Raven circles

round with eggs
Cedar Waxwing drinks and drinks
guardian mate close by

in a purple star-field
of gold-studded Asters two
Tarantulas mate

the Blood of Christ mountains
drink the sun all day — bleed
into sunset

in the Garden-Shrine
thirty-nine shades of green bower
the Red Clay Dish

splitting the fog,
San Pedro wears a morning cloak
of shimmering silk

dawn flame flicks along
the base of scudding clouds — topaz
in the Red Clay Dish

lavender and lemon Iris,
blue blue Bluebirds — nymphs
in the Garden Shrine

overnight cold snap —
Warbler bounces off the water
at the Red Clay Dish

a pilgrimage of Doves
settles at the Garden Shrine,
swapping Tales

black at twilight,
San Pedro and the Manzanos
anchor the sky

hot — Rabbit checks out
the Red Clay Dish: water low,
climbs in

a flock of Finches
swarms into the leafless Apple —
rosy, singing fruit

Karen paints two
flowering, sky-searching trees,
twined — us

white-tailed Rabbit
hops into a dawning sunbeam,
freezes — light sculpture

on the very top branch
of a Juniper, the Rose-finch
sings up a moon

twilight serenity
in the Garden Shrine — Jizo
and the twined love trees

the wind makes us crazy;
the birds power on — drop in for a drink
at the Red Clay Dish

tiny new Rabbit,
smaller than the passing Quail —
suns in the Garden Shrine

a stand of Iris
dances in the waters
of the Red Clay Dish

Doves calling
Flycatchers feasting
one blue crazy Butterfly

dawn, long silken clouds
open to the risen sun —
Leda :: The Swan

frigid air, searing sun,
a gentle wind bends the grass—
rattlesnake

red-gold Whip-snake
slips up out of a gopher hole,
checks the Red Clay Dish

under the blessing moon
a purple and an ivory Lilac
couple

Finch in the wind
snatches seeds from a rocking/
rolling Dahlia

mom and pop Quail
at the Red Clay Dish — twelve chicks
yesterday, three today

Bluebird wings
churn sun and water into
a jeweled belly-bath

no wind this morning
no birds no bouncing rabbits —
dead air

dim grey morning —
six dazzling Grosbeaks swoop into
the Red Clay Dish

moon-leached clouds cover
burned-out Jemez volcano —
snake skin in the garden

cloud of Ravens
pulses black over the arroyo
by the Red Clay Dish

Robin, rising sun,
gold burns in the water
of the Red Clay Dish

Robin and fledglings
splash & drink in the Red Clay Dish —
male guard stomps around

Ash Throated Flycatcher
downs a drink at the Red Clay Dish —
snaps up lunch, moves on

gale-force winds
twist the pines day and night —
the roots dig in

morning sun finds gold
in the rocks around San Pedro's
abandoned mines

in the Garden Shrine
new green pops into old gold grass —
presto, Rabbits

Sunday morning:
Orioles bathe, fluff, preen, prance —
the Red Clay Dish

baby Rabbit sits,
plunk, in the Red Clay Dish —
Jay storms in, baby runs

silver in sunlight
the Ring-necked Doves knit
a net of shadows

day after day, Falcon
returns to the Garden Shrine —
empties the Red Clay Dish

lone Robin lands,
scans, hops, pounces — food,
invisible

two Ravens circle, roll,
tumble, soar along San Pedro's
high snow ridges

fuzzy black Tarantula
strolls between Gay Feathers
around the Red Clay Dish

wind-ravaged Peonies
lift, bud, bloom, hover over
the Red Clay Dish

Red-shafted Flicker
bangs out a snack from the Elm
by the Red Clay Dish

yellow Daffodils,
facing the sun — beckon to
the Red Clay Dish

purple Hyacinth
in the Garden Shrine —
Indus valley god

three gaping beaks
in the Hummingbird nest —
Blue Jay prowls

new flock of Robins
grabs the tree; reigning Robin shrieks
jumps around — undone

wrangle for water
at the Red Clay Dish — Robin on
Robin on Robin

Easter — mating call
of the sweet-voiced Ring-neck Dove,
first Hyacinths

orange-red Lilies
disappear into the last rays
of a setting sun

dawn fire in the East,
lavender mist to the South —
hush at the Garden Shrine

frost — Bluebirds drop into
the Red Clay Dish, find a cup
of early morning ice

five drops of rain —
one iridescent Bluebird splashes
into the Red Clay Dish

always one goofball bird
squawking and charging — trying to own
the Red Clay Dish

the garden brown,
the air grit-brown — Sparrows skirmish
at the Red Clay Dish

night-ranging coyotes
flow to the water in the Red Clay Dish
— bone dry by morning

sun an ember
in ash-filled sky — Orioles blaze
in the Red Clay Dish

spring apple blossoms:
Prairie Fire, Indian Magic —
Wizards in the Garden Shrine

jewel-breasted Finch
gathers the sun, dunks it
in the Red Clay Dish

first flush of green
in the gold Shrine grasses —
St. Pat sneaks in

crescent moon sails
a flood tide of cloud — topaz,
coral, vermillion

the wind bangs on —
inside the wind is a cave,
inside that cave....

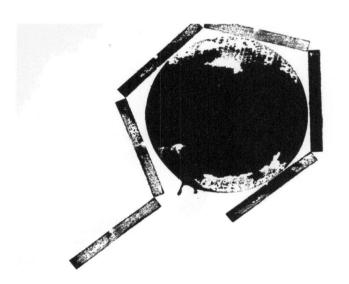

rising sun picks out
one small Rabbit's very big
pink transparent ears

Ring-necked Dove plump
among fat red berries and
scurrying ladybugs

hazy San Pedro—
just another giant cloud
above the Red Clay Dish

late sun finds three full-blown
double-pink, Last of Summer Roses
by the Red Clay Dish

early cold snap — the birds
twice as round but thin at the Rim Bar of
the Red Clay Dish

fall sunrise — San Pedro
draws a long, thin coral-cloak
over his bones

early morning tea —
by the last medley of Asian Lilies
in clear blue glass

the Red Clay Dish thaws;
Bluebirds and yellow Warbler sing
flounce, flutter

sunrise cold snap —
Finches, Sparrows, Warblers crowd in
at the Red Clay Dish

tiny yellow Warbler
lights on a wand of Crimson Bugler —
rides on the wind

Orioles in the olive tree
gather the dawn,
go gold

a guitar and a mountain —
which plays which
as the moon rises

lone Bluebird sits high
above the mountain Garden Shrine —
me on a hilltop, young

girl rabbit tries to graze,
guy rabbit wants to mate — looping
'round the Red Clay Dish

within white clouds,
tides of gold and silver —
on the page, three lines

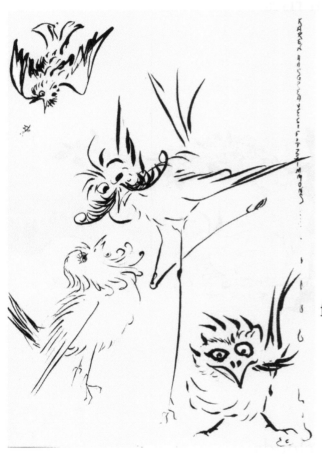

gaillards once prowled
the old Paris cafes — now lounge
'round the Red Clay Dish

smoke-laden morning —
a cascade of Waxwings floods
the Red Clay Dish

threading the garden
from pine to juniper to ash — the Wren
defines our Garden Shrine

soft long sweet rain,
Bluebirds, Swallows surf the air —
baby rabbits bounce

Mexican Jay scampers
over the grass, into a bush, up a tree, down
to the Red Clay Dish

quiet in the Shrine —
distant call of the Dove,
Hummingbird whir

in cloud and mist
big-shouldered San Pedro floats —
almost there

90 miles away
the blue Manzanos dissolve —
moonlight floats the garden

morning after morning
more, and more vivid, bird song —
the wind whispers, howls

quick dips/quick scans,
early Mourning Dove drinks slowly
from the Red Clay Dish

dusk — the liquid shape
of a young coyote browses the olives
by the Red Clay Dish

each year the Spring Snow
explodes into apple blossoms —
the spring winds then strip away

Hummingbird
drinks long at the Red Clay Dish —
never seen before

Venus and the Moon
canoodle in a cerulean sky —
dawn at the Garden Shrine

Crows gone —
Raven country now,
San Pedro peak

full moon setting,
slots into coral dawn haze
in the Rio Grande Gorge

some dawns explode,
some slip in, tease out the colors
of the Garden Shrine

early snow — Warbler
eyes a bowl of morning ice
at the Red Clay Dish

heavy snow,
the Shrine floats lightly on
a motionless sea

Red-breasted Sapsucker —
vivid at the snowed-in
ice-bound Red Clay Dish

sunrise Woodpecker,
scarlet hat, regal robe — Benediction
at the Red Clay Dish

jewel-winged Hummingbird
ravishes the Poppies
'round the Red Clay Dish

dawn Robin preens, struts,
drops in early at the Red Clay Dish —
no one to drink with

aloof on a branch
Townsend's Solitary eyes the crowd
at the Red Clay Dish

— hot —
Robin stretches out long and deep
in the Red Clay Dish

wind barrels in,
clouds gather, darken, thicken —
five drops of rain

drought hardens —
gophers, squirrels, rabbits,
swarm to the Red Clay Dish

a driving wind empties
the Red Clay Dish — of water,
birds, sky

Titmice skate, and peck at
the ice in the Red Clay Dish —
sun kicks in

snow on desert stone
builds to minarets and domes —
no camels, no bells

jeweled snow shrinks
around bronze and gold grasses —
slow dance of the roots

the snow layered Shrine
floats out to San Pedro peak
on a surf of cloud

Tulip, Lilly, Iris
break through in the Garden Shrine —
resurrection myths

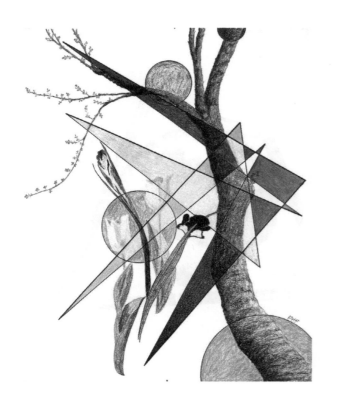

to weave her nest,
Robin dips a clutch of dry grass
into the Red Clay Dish

full-bore rain at last:
the Red Clay Dish is full —
San Pedro glows

dried-out Tumbleweed,
pale gold in the Garden Shrine —
trail of seeds

after the storm — whoosh,
a cascade of Waxwings drowns
the Red Clay Dish

San Pedro peak
absorbs the evening light, glows —
settles into sleep

a wash of white Iris
slips through the gold swells
of dry grasses

wind up, cold;
sun glides in, hot;
some kind of Tango

The Bar & Spa at The Red Clay Dish

how long can I sit
watching the Acts at The Red Clay Dish—
a long long, long long time

Robins strut, Bluebirds soar
Swallows twist and dive — Featured Acts
at The Red Clay Dish

clustered Autumn Joys,
soaring Gay Feathers — the Season
opens at The Red Clay Dish

wind plays
the strings of an ancient harp —
the dust dances

Orioles drinking at
the Rim-Bar of The Red Clay Dish—
one pops in

thwack whack — Flicker
drills for lunch in the Olive tree
above The Red Clay Dish

White-crowned Sparrow
preens, struts down the Runway
at The Red Clay Dish

nimble Yellow Warbler
bobbles for a drink at the Rim-Bar
of The Red Clay Dish

Morning Dove stops
for an evening bath and snack,
rejoins her song

Bullocks Oriole settles
at the Bar of The Red Clay Dish—
celestial harlequin

purple Gay Feathers
prance with Lazuli Bunting
'round The Red Clay Dish

Swainson's Hawk
powers down — broad-ribbed wings
dwarf The Red Clay Dish

dusky Tufted Titmouse,
suave in a swarm of squabbling Sparrows
struts at The Red Clay Dish

plump showy Quail
breaks her fast with an early drink
at The Red Clay Dish

having a bath,
drinking the bath water — Robins get down
at The Red Clay Dish

dazzling in blue,
Pinyon Jay checks out the action
at The Red Clay Dish

Flycatcher and Finch
line-dance at the Rim Bar
of The Red Clay Dish

elegant, edgy
Ring-necked Dove drinks one quick shot
at The Red Clay Dish

Evening Grosbeak swings
his bronze-black elegance into the dance
at The Red Clay Dish

a spray of Penstemon
backs the white-cloud/blue-sky tango
at The Red Clay Dish

Scarlet Buglers sway
with the singers at the Rim-Bar
of The Red Clay Dish

Curved-Bill Thrasher
drinks at The Red Clay Dish— snaps up
a passing lunch, moves on

frock-coated Robin
rolls up, parks, presents his card
at The Red Clay Dish

a gang of Robins
muscles into The Red Clay Dish
Finches, Wrens exit

Red-bellied Woodpecker
thumps his drum high above the circle-dance
at The Red Clay Dish

the Swallows swoop, spin
soar — no time for the Hop
at The Red Clay Dish

gauzy filaments
of wild Asparagus bid welcome
to The Red Clay Dish

Scarlet-headed Finch
squabbles with a Blue-winged Warbler — both
bow to The Red Clay Dish

stunning in black
the Cowbird flips off her name at the Bar
of The Red Clay Dish

Quantum Quirks at The Red Clay Dish

Harry Potter's head
rocks on the rim of The Red Clay Dish —
the Ravens gather, stare

Titmouse shakes,
shimmies in the full-again Red Clay Dish —
happy little drunk

Cowbird stops for a bath
at The Red Clay Dish — hangs her
six-gun on a branch

Towhee fledgling hops,
peers into The Red Clay Dish —
Crocs?

Crow, loud in the middle
of the dried-up Red Clay Dish —
Speaker of the House

Spells & Curses —
Harry Potter breaks the bank
at The Red Clay Dish

two resident Finches: —
with tall tree, low perch, seeds, water,
cell-phone somewhere

dreams of being chased
by an axe-waving, dry cackling
furious Red Clay Dish

fresh batch of Robins —
dogfights and hot pursuits at
The Red Clay Dish

"Red Baron" hummer
jumps the Lucifer — dogfight
over The Red Clay Dish

Karen comes down:
blue shirt, white pants — ready to sail
The Red Clay Dish

an ant on the window —
an elephant in the garden, hippos
in The Red Clay Dish

The Mountain Garden Shrine

white Shrine lantern,
rooted in earth, lifts to heaven —
satori

Gambel's Quail catch some sun
at the Garden Shrine — dip and drink,
stretch and fly

five Titmice cluster
in the Red Clay Dish — Hawk shadow,
gone

scarlet Finches gather
along the tops of the highest trees —
small suns

quiet in the Shrine —
far call of the mating doves,
Hummingbird whir

morning after wild winds
the birds fly in from everywhere —
to a dry Red Clay Dish

just barely there
through smoke and dust —
San Pedro still tames the demons

two large Quail lead
10 fuzzy little balls with legs —
come back next day alone

mist-held Sangres —
roll up to heaven, jumbled,
massive, feathery

puffed up, sun-breasted
Bluebird, perched high and cold,
calls in the dawn

melting hoarfrost
pours a dazzle of sun shards
into the Red Clay Dish

Sun plays the grasses,
Jizo and the lantern smile —
in the Garden Shrine

wide-eyed raven at dusk
black in the green of the olive tree,
watches us watching him

San Pedro hunkers
round; every gully, ridge and crag
wiped out by smoke

not a single bird,
rabbit, lizard, snake, this morning —
the Red Clay Dish dry

San Pedro at dawn
wears a shimmering purple cloak of
Bosque wildfire haze

swift White-tailed Rabbit
sprints, twirls, circles, jumps —
Mercury

showy Butterfly
courts itself in the sun-bright,
mirror window

San Pedro mountain
floats its plundered mines high
above the Friars' trail

yellow Dutch Tulips
speckle the green sweep of the Shrine —
sun chalices

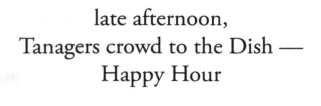

late afternoon,
Tanagers crowd to the Dish —
Happy Hour

at the Garden Shrine
Quail and Rabbits disappear
four Coyotes amble through

Ravens slice across
a steely North Sea sky — Bombers
1943

dry country dawn —
smell the wind, call in the clouds,
memorize the rain

cold ghost of a wind
runs its fingers through the grasses
of the Garden Shrine

both Doves fly in,
settle high in the Olive tree —
grace the Garden Shrine

cloud and light play —
the opening and closing of
Siddhartha's eyes

rollicking wind,
rocking and rolling shrine trees —
tea and biscuits

our Canyon Towhees
do their old-couple thing —
never far apart

birdsong pauses as
Karen plants a rose for Skelly,
quiet in his grave

day after the kill
of his mate and chick, the Dove
circles and calls — calls

White-tail bunny
scurries after a browsing
plump Towhee — Mom?

sun-drenched morning,
the Garden Shrine empty —
silence, space, small winds

sunrise high
on drifting cathedral domes,
translucent chapels

Hyacinth: dying
and resurrecting Hindu god —
no cross, no nails

purple Butterfly bush —
born again in the overflow
of the Red Clay Dish

the rising sun
strikes the Garden Shrine lantern —
ignites the stone

scarlet Bugler-penstemon
bobs and sways; Hummingbird hovers,
aims — bulls eye

late fall joins
a wiry wine-red Barberry
and a dying Dahlia

male and female Finch
side by side on the seed-log
feed, nuzzle

all the birds are back
bluebirds, robins, titmice, finch —
bathing & squabbling

hanging Wisteria
catch the setting sun —
purple rain

early Robin preens,
master of the Red Clay Dish,
he thinks

wild asparagus
in the summer wind — five feet tall,
dancing

eyeball to eyeball
Finch and Sparrow negotiate
water rights

pearl-grey Doves,
a couple, a suitor — Opera
at the Shrine

sun sets — Shrine lantern
and Father Hugo roses
beam at each other

clouds blur San Pedro,
fog slips over the Garden Shrine
— one Woodpecker

rustle and scurry
of something tiny in the grass —
Nighthawk flashes in

Quail and Wrens
browse by the Red Clay Dish — gone;
four Coyotes amble in

black San Pedro
muscles into a clear dawn sky —
Ravens at the Shrine

crescent moon sails
a fire-tide of cloud — topaz,
coral, vermillion

bronze and blue Iris
hover over the Red Clay Dish —
stars in the sun

first long rain,
Finches, Bluebirds, Swallows sail —
baby rabbits bounce

monsoon, monsoon,
true monsoon — heart swells, mind
prances with the rain

in the noon window —
a Mountain, a Bluebird, the Shrine,
a Fly

dazzle of bees
on the Spring-Snow blossoms —
spring concerto

one scarlet Tulip
in freshly turned black earth —
Garden Shrine essence

banquet of small fruit —
Bluebirds feast high — coyotes
party in the grass

mist and cloud hang
in the clefts of San Pedro peak —
Japan

birds chasing birds
rabbits chasing rabbits —
what's a boy to do

small wind, no birds —
the Garden Shrine hums
its morning mantra

on each Iris petal
a little golden beard —
on San Pedro, gold clouds

this morning's dawn
opens San Pedro like a rose —
petals, folds, color

cold,
one last cicada at sunset —
counting down

icy morning wind
swirls spiders of new snow
around the Red Clay Dish

domes of spring snow
fluffed and puffed the Garden Shrine
— upended wells

jaunty cap of snow
on the stone shrine lantern — snow melt
sweetens the grasses

wine-crimson Dahlia,
sundown beacon by the side
of the Red Clay Dish

full fall rain,
heavy and cold until just sunset —
golden water seeds

San Pedro mountain
floats on a long white stretch of cloud —
dinosaur feather

first snow on San Pedro
magick's the whole sunlit Garden Shrine
and the Red Clay Dish

Scarlet Tanagers,
one last drink at the Red Clay Dish —
south

rain swallows the hills,
sun tumbles along the cactus —
on the path, lizards mate

full sunlight
after a night of wind-whipped rain —
the sunflowers stretch

one full-blown Dahlia,
one unborn Dahlia in a bud —
morning coffee

less smoke, more wings,
the setting sun slants in golden —
the Nighthawks strum

alone on the trail
through the mountain Garden Shrine —
three gaunt coyote pups

San Pedro comes and goes
in thick wildfire smoke — Whale
in a breaking sea

dry months\dry winds —
Bluebird and Grackle pace the deck
of the Red Clay Dish

Peace
in the Garden Shrine this morning —
Krishna in the blossoms

fresh snow on cloud-clutched
San Pedro punches up a new range
— dwarf Alps

Toreador winds
whip the Veronica Blue Queens
to a ritual dance

under black clouds
the Garden Shrine grasses still
somehow glow

two trees, two Robins,
two trees, four Robins sunning
fifth Robin — riot!

by the Shrine lantern
a constellation of new Cinquefoil
winks in the dark

Chrysanthemums
growing out of his head,
Jizo smiles and smiles

the Prairie Grasses
dance differently with the wind —
each its own elegance

no birds this morning,
not one —
a storm of Crows

rain at last —
sophisticated gardener Karen
flings a demented jig

San Pedro rolls out
black from rosy morning fog —
wind and birds asleep

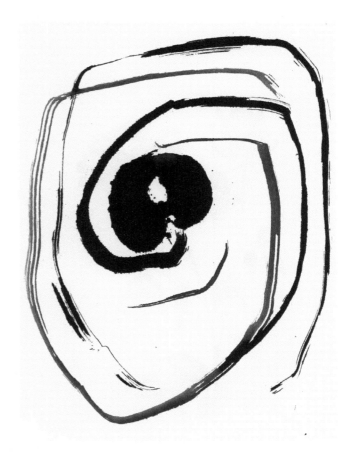

Rufous-backed Robin
up from Mexico muscles into
the Red Clay Dish

three Tea Roses
float in clear turquoise water —
spring tinted clouds, high

stone Shrine lantern
in a tangle of prairie grasses —
moonlit mountains soar

Hummingbird holds still
on the top of a thin green branch
a full five seconds

the far Manzanos
in a sunset haze of pink and orange —
a song

the world dips,
captures the morning sun —
unveils the Shrine

above the Red Clay Dish
San Pedro rides a rising wave —
breaking blue hills

copper winter grass
in a lace of new blue snow —
pine whipping gale

winds in the snow-choked
Sangre de Cristo passes —
pioneer whispers

sun-filled Hibiscus
by Jizo's head — a smile as wide
as his own

Jizo peers 'round
the bottle, winks his third eye —
opens mine

Chrysanthemum
growing out of his head, Jizo
cocks his eye — your turn

the sun sets later,
the stars burn brighter —
soon, Blake's Tiger

Dove chick down; parents
coax, feed, shelter — next day
small feathers everywhere

Ring-necked Dove, caught
in a stormy Northeast wind, flips,
soars, spins, glides

Doves nest again in
the *portal* vine tangle where
last year's chick was killed

the great heat gone —
pearlescent clouds, crystal skies
the Garden Shrine

west wind huffs, puffs,
trees, grasses bow, let it go —
Tao

red Autumn Joys
float in a field of rain-fresh grasses,
yellow Paper Flowers

December sun slips
into an icy purple sky —
Apache Plums ignite

caught in a tangle
of old roses, dawn floods the scree
of burnished copper leaves

the Sun has his way
with grasses, flowers, and trees —
juice all around

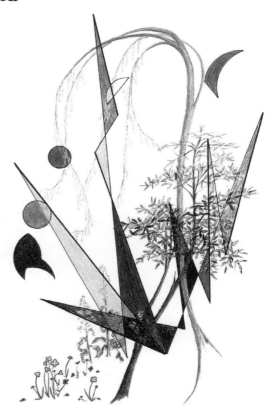

perched
on the garden's stone shrine-lantern
two Doves mate — again

San Pedro's muscles
flex black around fine jeweled snow —
wrestle the sun

the long ridges roll
from San Pedro to the Manzanos —
high desert tides

quiet riot
of Peonies and daffodils —
pot of tea

purple-black skies —
one sliver of silver radiance
along San Pedro's flank

night storm's outriders
drum on the skin of the house —
sleep hides

lean, weatherbeaten
old San Pedro peak returns
at dawn — in pink

year's first plum blossoms —
small leaves, smaller petals,
same mind sweeping scent

wind-ravaged bird house,
perky bright yellow chicks —
village housing

the Garden tilts East,
finds the sun, slips into
a coat of many colors

the Robbin swoops in first
then the whole winged village
pecks the ice, waits for the sun

Us

Karen —
every evening, sunset,
every morning, you

before I met you
I did not have a heart — it had
shriveled up and died

the dry wind blows,
the rain don't rain — still,
her flowers grow

every morning
in Karen's mountain Garden Shrine
I find myself

Warblers dip and bow —
wind and water play with heaven
in the Red Clay Dish

Yellow Warbler flickers
in the dark of the pines —
breaks out to the Red Clay Dish

hard rain and hail —
the setting sun trails a haze of gold
over the Garden Shrine

between the candles
the setting sun slips down
into our wine glasses

lamplight before dawn —
Karen's paintings float off the walls,
whispering

from Karen's hands
clouds of iris and peonies rise,
float on their own scent

during the night
her tulips pop open — morning tea
with small moon bursts

of Venus and the Moon,
Keeper of the Garden Shrine —
my salvation

first green in the garden,
dawn inflames San Pedro peak —
I first meet Karen

early spring — Karen seeds
a constellation of grace
into the coming fall

Karen has lined stones
along our long garden paths
into serenity

thin winter branches
lift black into an azure sky —
Karen's zen paintings

sun on her bed,
Megan makes the three magic circles —
settles in

cold floor this morning —
long dog Megan curls up round
on my slippered feet

early toast and tea
and Megan's big brown eyes —
to treat or not to treat

dawn — coyote comes,
Megan explodes, twirls, barks, snarls,
coyote saunters off

dance of the trees
in a dry Southwest Rockies gale —
wild days at sea

Oregon Juncos flock
to the seeds above the Red Clay Dish —
drop in to sip some snow

San Pedro gathers clouds
to lift it higher than itself —
the sun too

snow dust on dry grass,
black branches whip at clouds —
winter!

tiny Bewick's Wrens
play hopscotch in the seeds
'round the Red Clay Dish

Hummingbird browses
a blossom-buffet — sip of this,
sip of that, whoosh

floating in the incense
of a high-desert cloudburst —
Karen's Garden Shrine

a wave of Chickadees
floods the Red Clay Dish — drinks, bathes
flows on

Karen kneels to new green
in winter's brown dry jumble —
cleans, channels the sun

the far Manzanos
brought close and massive through
a lens of frozen mist

2013: San Pedro
burns white through a surf
of magenta cloud

within their music
the Ring-necked Doves glide and soar
above the Red Clay Dish

Hawk soars overhead,
Megan decodes rocks and grass —
I link earth and sky

coffee and Danish
by the Red Clay Dish — good dog Megan
by my side drooling

Megan
draped over the sunny side of the couch,
golden face, amber eyes

thunder grumble, growls,
lightening strobes and slashes —
Megan snoozes

Robins chasing Robins,
Rabbits chasing Rabbits — Megan
sits, enthralled

Megan reads the garden,
I scan a wall of idling books —
Yeats, Baudelaire, Blake....

working the garden,
Karen kneels — Megan hovers, scans,
never far

Megan's garden cruise:
from sun-drenched isle to shaded cove —
no tickets, no plan

I scratch her ears —
Megan sings a love song
deep in her chest

pileup of clouds
thins the morning sun — Megan
and I get what we can

new leaves all around
Karen throws, Megan catches,
I step on Megan's foot

Megan stalks the wee lizards
that quicksilver the Garden Shrine
bliss in motion

sun on Megan's face
slips along high bone ridges,
circles into gold

Megan's hip, my hip, both
bad today; she wants a rub —
helps her, helps me

Megan hunts lizards
through grass around the Red Clay Dish:
none! — gets some sun

Rocky Mountain bunny
drinks long from the Red Clay Dish —
Megan drools

red rock, red clay, red dirt —
the Sangre de Cristos burn
in the noonday sun

brave Hummingbird
flits in, out of the spray
at the Red Clay Dish

pink on the Sedum, copper
on the Vines — Scarlet Tanager
at the Red Clay Dish

the Stargazer Lily
offers us six fleshy petals
one giant pistil

walking by water,
sun in one hand, moon in the other,
cross the stream

San Pedro peak
burns white in an evening surf
of magenta cloud

pine calligraphy
in a brightening mauve sky — dawn
at the Garden Shrine

a wild gale drives away
every bird — each with its
singular small song

sucking in the sap
from the all around round —
pulsing out poems

first sunbeam slips in
through a stack of dismal cloud —
the Shrine explodes

daybreak, crystal peaks —
poised on a shimmering cactus,
one yellow Warbler

Hibiscus blossoms
die into tight, swirled elegance —
still offering pollen

slow swelling sun
slips over dense white cloud — first
words on a blank page

each morning new Flax
fresh Hyacinths, new Tulips —
new light in her eyes

snow dresses San Pedro
in white silk — sunrise
adds the jewels

Karen's table stones —
desert mountain range, brooding Owl,
Tigers poised....

reading the rain
with Karen — maker and keeper
of the Garden Shrine

crippled Megan barks,
drives off three coyotes —
smiles

sunset rain unlocks
the withered high desert soil —
Arabian spice

dawn after rain —
a wash of gold acknowledges
the Garden Shrine

end of day,
sun on his face,
moon in her eyes

Karen and Thomas have lived much of their lives in other countries, including 10 years on and off in Japan. In the mid-1970s they did a 16 month, 18 nation poetry-performance\lecturing\workshops tour through the Western Pacific, South Asia, the Middle East and Europe under the auspices of the United States Information Service (USIS) and the State Department. They have for 25 years published, for distribution by University of Hawai'i Press, a series of modern Japanese poets in translation (30 volumes), and another series that considers and reflects Japanese aesthetics.

While in Japan, Karen studied oriental brush painting with a Japanese master and now teaches it here. She also works in western modes — oil, watercolor, pastel, collage, monoprint. Thomas has written, translated, and edited a large number of books. They live in the Rockies just south of Santa Fe, New Mexico.